SPOTLIGHT ON SOCIAL AND EMOTIONAL LEARNING

ACTING WITH AWARENESS

RESPECT FOR OTHERS

LISA IDZIKOWSKI

PowerKiDS press™

NEW YORK

Published in 2020 by The Rosen Publishing Group, Inc.
29 East 21st Street, New York, NY 10010

Editor: Elizabeth Krajnik
Designer: Michael Flynn

Photo Credits: Cover asiseeit/E+/Getty Images; cover, pp. 1, 3–8, 10–12, 14, 16–18; 20–24 (background) TairA/Shutterstock.com; p. 4 Brocreative/Shutterstock.com; p. 5 Iakov Filimonov/Shutterstock.com; p. 6 Syda Productions/Shutterstock.com; p. 7 LightField Studios/Shutterstock.com; p. 9 David M. Benett/Getty Images Entertainment/Getty Images; p. 10 Jacob Lund/Shutterstock.com; p. 11 E. Charbonneau/WireImage/Getty Images; p. 13 Courtesy of the Library of Congress; p. 15 Mike Ehrmann/Getty Images Sport/Getty Images; p. 16 Alfa Photostudio/Shutterstock.com; p. 17 Jose Luis Pelaez Inc/DigitalVision/Getty Images; p. 19 Mandy Godbehear/Shutterstock.com; p. 20 altanaka/Shutterstock.com; p. 21 Dmytro Zinkevych/Shutterstock.com; p. 22 glenda/Shutterstock.com.

Cataloging-in-Publication Data

Names: Idzikowski, Lisa.
Title: Acting with awareness: respect for others / Lisa Idzikowski.
Description: New York : PowerKids Press, 2020. | Series: Spotlight on social and emotional learning | Includes glossary and index.
Identifiers: ISBN 9781725306493 (pbk.) | ISBN 9781725306523 (library bound) | ISBN 9781725306509 (6pack)
Subjects: LCSH: Respect for persons--Juvenile literature. | Etiquette for children and teenagers--Juvenile literature.
Classification: LCC BJ1533.R42 I37 2020 | DDC 179'.9--dc23

Manufactured in the United States of America

CPSIA Compliance Information: Batch #CWPK20. For further information contact Rosen Publishing, New York, New York at 1-800-237-9932.

CONTENTS

CHAPTER ONE

RESPECT FOR ALL

In the morning, your dad asks what you want for lunch. At school, your friend asks you if you're doing OK. At recess, your teacher listens as you tell her about a problem you have with another student. Your mom **compliments** you for doing well on a school project. These are all ways people show respect. However, respect isn't just how other people treat you. You should respect the people around you, too. You should also respect yourself.

Being kind to your server when you go out to eat is respectful. You should listen to the server carefully and say "please" and "thank you."

Knowing what is and isn't respect can sometimes be tricky. Different people and **cultures** have different ways of showing respect. Sometimes, people do things they think are respectful, but other people don't agree. This book will help you understand what respect is, how to show it, and why it's important.

CHAPTER TWO

WHAT IS RESPECT?

Respect means different things to different people. These things often have qualities in common, however. Respect is when you act in a way that shows you're aware of someone's rights, wishes, values, beliefs, and culture. It's good to show respect to the people you interact with on a regular basis.

The Golden Rule says you should treat people the way you want to be treated. If you were being bullied, what would you want your friends to do?

Respect for others is a type of social awareness. Social awareness is when you can think about things from other people's point of view—even if they're different from you—and **empathize** with them. Respecting others will help you appreciate **diversity**. However, to respect others, you must first respect yourself. You can practice self-respect by thinking about the things you're good at. Making sure your own needs are met is another way of practicing self-respect.

CHAPTER THREE

COOL TO BE KIND

Have you ever seen a family member share a treat, such as a batch of yummy, fresh-baked brownies, with a neighbor? Does your teacher greet you when you come into his classroom? Have you ever sent someone a nice email, letter, or text message? People who are respectful are often said to be friendly, kind, and considerate.

Being respectful also means saying you're sorry (and meaning it) when you do or say something disrespectful. You might have said something rude to someone without really thinking about it. Maybe you said something like, "Your hair is so messy today!" Even if you say you're sorry **sincerely**, the person may still be upset. However, you should still say you're sorry.

Thinking about your words and being respectful often take practice. You can practice by thinking about other people's points of view and how they might feel.

Taylor Swift is known for being a famous singer and songwriter. However, she's also known for being kind and **donating** her time and money to help people.

CHAPTER FOUR

KEEP IT POSITIVE

Sometimes, respect includes being positive about other people. But it's not always easy to be positive. Sometimes we don't like or agree with other people. Maybe a classmate is saying things you feel are wrong, or maybe your younger brother is bugging you. You can be respectful even when things like this happen. Listen to your classmate, but respectfully say how you feel, too. Consider that your brother really wants your attention. You might have to work extra hard to stay positive sometimes.

If you and your friend are trying to learn how to play guitar, staying positive can help your friend stay positive. It also shows your friend that you are respectful of their feelings.

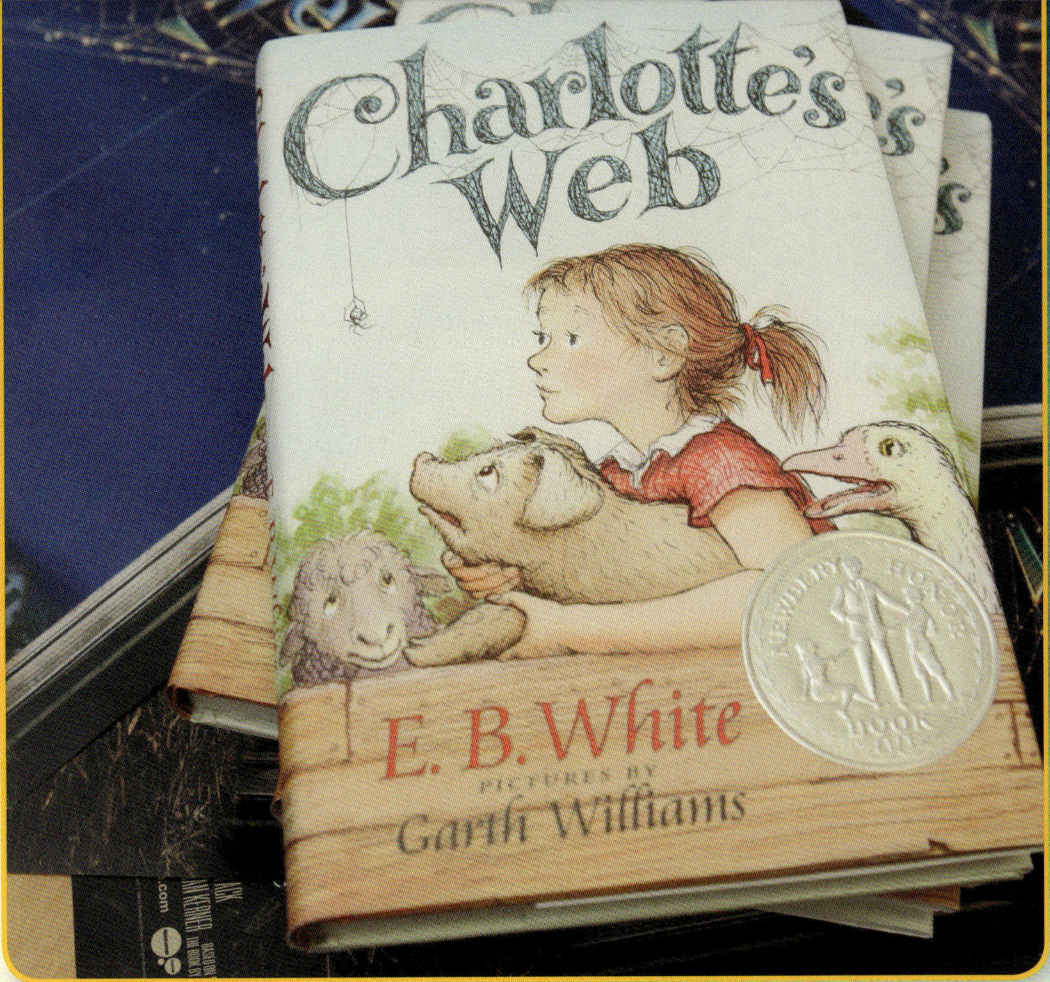

You can help other people stay positive, too, by being positive about them. In the book *Charlotte's Web*, Charlotte calls Wilbur "some pig," "terrific," and other nice things. She wants to help him feel better about himself and to help others think positive things about him, too. Speaking about someone respectfully helps them stay positive when things aren't going well.

CHAPTER FIVE

THE BEAUTY OF DIFFERENCES

Everyone is unique, or one of a kind. We all have likes and dislikes. People eat different foods, listen to different music, wear different clothes, and do many other different things. Appreciating diversity is another way of showing social awareness and being respectful of others.

Part of respect is **tolerance**. If you're respectful, you understand that people have many differences and that's a good thing! It's respectful to accept and try to understand these differences, such as different religions, different cultures, different appearances, and different likes and dislikes.

Tolerance doesn't mean accepting some bad choices or behavior, though. If your friend cheats on a math test, you shouldn't tolerate that. Tell a teacher! Bullies shouldn't be tolerated, either. Don't accept things that hurt people.

Respect is also treating people well no matter how much money they have. Scientist Albert Einstein once said, "I speak to everyone in the same way, whether he is the garbageman or the president of the university."

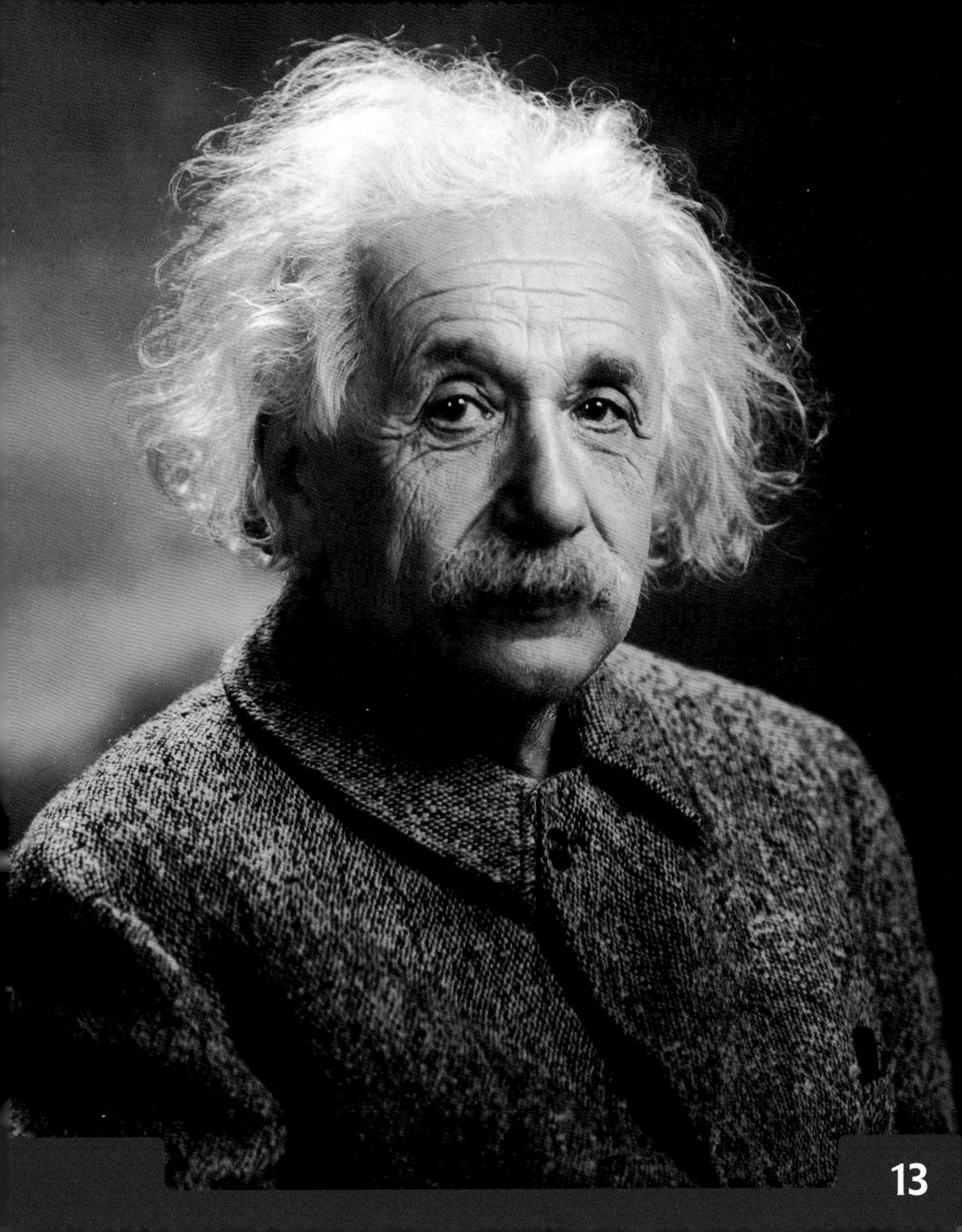

CHAPTER SIX

BEING A GOOD SPORT

Do you play sports? Respect is important in sports, too. It doesn't matter if you're a soccer player or a skier, a basketball player or a bowler, or an Olympic or high school **athlete**. You should play fair, follow the rules, listen to your coaches and other officials, and treat teammates and other players with respect. This is called sportsmanship.

No matter how good an athlete you are, you probably won't win all the time. What happens when you lose? Do you cry or scream at your coach? Do you say bad things about the other team? Of course not!

Being a good sport is a way of showing respect for others. Give members of the winning team a high five. Shake hands with the tennis player who beat you. **Congratulate** the runner who won the race. It feels good to win, but it's more important to show respect for others and have fun!

At the 2014 Winter Olympics in Sochi, Russia, Torah Bright (right), an Australian snowboarder, gave a pep talk to Kelly Clark (left), a snowboarder from the United States, after she saw Clark was upset. Clark ended up beating Bright, but Bright was the first to congratulate Clark after her silver-medal run.

USA

CHAPTER SEVEN

LEND A HAND

Do your parents ever ask you to help out around the house? Do you take out the trash, wash the dishes, or look after your younger brother or sister? At school, do you keep your desk clean, take care of a class pet, or turn off the computers at the end of the day? If you do, this is being respectful, too!

Volunteering to serve meals to the homeless is a great way to connect with people in your community. People in need deserve your respect, too!

You can also show respect for people by helping out in your community. Many groups could use your help. People, families, and school groups often **volunteer** in their communities. You could do a number of things, such as helping in after-school programs, senior centers, and soup kitchens. Some people tutor students who need help in school. Others spend time with people in the hospital. Some people walk dogs at an animal shelter. Volunteering is a way to show you respect your community and other people.

CHAPTER EIGHT

GIVE A COMPLIMENT

Everyone feels bad from time to time. Respectful people will find a way to help others feel better. Do you have a classmate who didn't get picked to play on a kickball team at recess? What about a friend who didn't get asked to the school dance?

When someone is feeling sad or upset, sometimes even a small thing can help them feel better. You can brighten their day by giving them a genuine, or real, compliment. You could tell your classmate, "You're a great friend." This will show them you really care about them. Both giving and getting compliments can help you and others feel good!

It might feel strange to give a compliment. However, you can learn this social skill by practicing! The best compliments are those about something the person can control.

Genuine compliments can be a way of showing respect. The more you give compliments, the more likely you are to receive them in return.

CHAPTER NINE

RESPECTING NATURE

Many people, including friends, family, teachers, and community members, deserve respect. Nature also deserves our respect. Earth is home to all kinds of living creatures. It and they need to be protected and respected. Without plants, we wouldn't have food or air to breathe. Without animals, the environment, or the natural world around us, would fall apart.

Your community may have special rules for recycling. Ask an adult to help you check these rules.

Have you learned about the three Rs—reduce, reuse, recycle—in school? We need to reduce, or lessen, how much waste we make. This means using things again instead of throwing them away. It also means using things for as long as possible and repairing them if they break. We should also find new uses for things, such as turning an old kitchen table into a work station instead of throwing it away. Some items, such as cardboard and plastic products, should be recycled to make new products.

CHAPTER TEN

WHY BE RESPECTFUL?

Why should you be respectful? Being respectful is an important social skill because it shows other people you care enough about them to think about their feelings and experiences. Doing things such as saying "thank you" to a crossing guard who helps you or being kind to a cashier at the grocery store are small acts of respect that can have a big effect. Being respectful encourages people to show respect to others, too.

People aren't perfect. Sometimes we forget to be respectful, or we may get upset with someone and say something we don't mean. Fortunately, there's a good way to remember how to be respectful to others. The Golden Rule tells us to treat others as we would want to be treated. Be kind, tolerant, helpful, and a good sport. Try to keep a positive view. Give genuine compliments often and take care of Earth. You'll feel good about it!

GLOSSARY

athlete (ATH-leet) A person who is trained in or good at games or exercises that require physical skill, endurance, and strength.

compliment (KAHM-pluh-muhnt) To say nice things about someone or something. Also, something good someone says about someone or something.

congratulate (kuhn-GRAA-chuh-layt) To tell someone you're happy for them.

culture (KUHL-chuhr) The beliefs and ways of life of a certain group of people.

diversity (duh-VUHR-suh-tee) The quality or state of having many different types, forms, or ideas.

donate (DOH-nayt) To give something in order to help a person or group.

empathize (EM-puh-thyz) To understand and share the same feelings as another person.

sincerely (sin-SEER-lee) In a genuine, or real, way.

tolerance (TAH-luh-ruhnts) Willingness to accept other ideas, beliefs, or points of view.

volunteer (vah-luhn-TEER) To do something to help because you want to do it.

INDEX

PRIMARY SOURCE LIST

Page 9
Taylor Swift switches on the Christmas lights at Westfield London. Photograph. David M. Benett. November 6, 2012. Getty Images Entertainment via Getty Images.

Page 13
Albert Einstein. Photograph. Orren Jack Turner. ca. 1947. Now kept at the Library of Congress Prints and Photographs Division, Washington, D.C.

Page 15
Torah Bright at the ladies' snowboard cross quarterfinals. Mike Ehrmann. February 12, 2014. Getty Images Sport via Getty Images.

WEBSITES

Due to the changing nature of Internet links, PowerKids Press has developed an online list of websites related to the subject of this book. This site is updated regularly. Please use this link to access the list: www.powerkidslinks.com/SSEL/respect